PRAISE FOR
CABBAGE TO LEMONADE?

"Tina Hunt and I have known each other as members of the North Carolina Native American Lumbee Tribe. As a retired educator, I find Tina to be a dedicated advocate for our tribe. She has a story to tell as she deals with health issues. Tina is self-employed and works diligently to share her knowledge, skills, and talents not only in her church and community but throughout North Carolina and nearby areas. Get to know a beautiful Native American girl as she tells a beautiful story."

—**DELLA REVELS HARTIS**

"Tina and I have been friends for many years. Her father and I are friends and fishing buddies. I found this book to be relatable to everyday life. At some point in life, we will all encounter situations found in this book."

—**BYRON DAVIS,** Pastor of Liberation Ministries

"I've been fortunate to know Tina and her family for over 20 years as a coworker, friend, and patient. Don't let Tina's size and sweet disposition fool you. She's like a five-ton bulldozer when she's got a goal and mission in mind, and you definitely don't want to get in her way. Her loyalty to family, friends, and herself is unmatched. She's faced more challenges than most people I know, yet she's taken that cabbage and made gold. Thank you for being such a great inspiration. I hope many others can benefit from her incredible story."

—**ROYCE R. SYRACUSE,** MD, MBA

"Although the narrative revolves around Tina's life story, the book is extremely motivational and leads you to engage with and self-reflect on your own life. I really appreciated how she has been able to take some of the simplest things and make an analogy that provokes thought and spiritual revelation. This book will be hard to put down and promote feelings of encouragement and self-determination."

—**MITZY PARKER-SANDERS,** high school classmate of Tina, the mighty Viking of North Mecklenburg class of 1984

"Tina Hunt was a student in my class back in the 80s at North Mecklenburg High School. I was her Health Occupations Education teacher, and Tina wanted to pursue a medical career after high school. So, my class was the perfect elective for her. This little dynamo had a heart as big as Dallas, Texas, and a 'can do' spirit that reached the clouds even back then. Her sweet soul has not changed! A naturally precious character was present even when Tina was medically challenged over and over and over again. Anyone else would have given up and thrown in the towel... but not Tina. The title of this book is just awesome, and it describes this woman to a 'T!' She can circumvent any situation and make it better. Her out-of-the-box thinking will have her leaving NO stone unturned to reach a goal or help someone else reach a goal. In the end, the mission was accomplished in a different way from the way others would approach the situation. I love the title and cannot wait to read the entire book! As I read my assigned reading portion... I could hear Tina's voice... She was in the room with me as I read it. It made me smile."

—**CONNIE WINGERT-BAKER**

"Tina, I am incredibly proud of you. You have indeed overcome numerous obstacles in your lifetime. I love the way you took an example of a trip to the grocery store and then shared many experiences of what God can do when we give Him our goals. Even when things don't go as we hoped, we also learn to 'take cabbage and make lemonade.'"

—**GWENDOLYN HUNT LOCKLEAR,** Aunt

Cabbage to Lemonade?

Cabbage to Lemonade?

Turning Life's Obstacles into Opportunities

TINA HUNT

Copyright © 2024 by Tina Hunt

All rights reserved. No part of this book may be reproduced or transmitted in any form or by any means, electronic or mechanical, including photocopying, recording, any information storage, and retrieval system, without the written permission of the author, except for brief quotations embodied in critical articles and reviews.

For information on distribution rights, royalties, derivative works, or licensing opportunities on behalf of this content or work, please contact the publisher at the address below:

Farmhouse Publishings, LLC
P.O. Box 333
Spearfish, SD 57783

Scripture quotations from *The Authorized (King James) Version*. Rights in the Authorized Version in the United Kingdom are vested in the Crown. Reproduced by permission of the Crown's patentee, Cambridge University Press.

Scripture quotations marked (NIV) are taken from THE HOLY BIBLE, NEW INTERNATIONAL VERSION®. Copyright© 1973, 1978, 1984, 2011 by Biblica, Inc.™. Used by permission of Zondervan.

Although the author and publisher have tried to ensure that the information and advice in this book were correct and accurate at press time, the author and publisher do not assume and disclaim any liability to any party for any loss, damage, or disruption caused by acting upon the information in this book or by errors or omissions, whether such errors or omissions result from negligence, accident, or any other cause.

ISBN (Softcover): 979-8-9881344-9-7
ISBN (Ebook): 979-8-9906020-0-7

Design by Heidi Caperton
Editing by Kendra Paulton

Printed in the United States of America

TABLE OF CONTENTS

Chapter 1: Introduction 1

Chapter 2: Who Is Tina Hunt? 5

Chapter 3: Ingredients Needed 9

Chapter 4: Cabbage Number One – The Diagnosis . . . 13

Chapter 5: Cabbage Number Two – College
Opportunities with Determination 19

Chapter 6: Cabbage Number Three – The Fall with
"I Can" and "I Will". 25

Chapter 7: Cabbage Number Four – Will I Ever
Walk Again? 31

Chapter 8: Give Up, Give In, or Give It Your All 37

Chapter 9: Cabbage Number Five - Shocked
and Scared 45

Chapter 10: The Call 49

Chapter 11: Cabbage Number Six - Where Did This
Cabbage Come From? 57

Chapter 12: Cabbage Number Seven - Find a Way,
Make a Way 61

Chapter 13: Cabbage Number Eight - The Transition . . 67

Chapter 14: How to Live Without My Mom 71

Chapter 15: Cabbage Number Nine - What's
Happening? 77

Chapter 16: The Heart of Faith over Fear. 83

Chapter 17: Make Some Lemonade 89

Chapter 18: Do Not Judge by What You See 93

Chapter 19: Broken For A Purpose 97

Resources 101

About the Author 115

Introduction

Have you ever gone to the grocery store and purchased items for a specific recipe just to get home and realize you have forgotten something? Or better yet, while preparing the dish, you realize that it will not be enough and you need to double the recipe, but you don't have enough ingredients, and the grocery store is closed? Personally, I avoid going to the grocery stores late at night.

This happened to me this year for Easter. I went to the grocery store on the Thursday before Easter to purchase the ingredients for the dish I was preparing. Although I love people and I talk to everyone, to go to the grocery store on the weekend of a big holiday… Well, I will pass on that one.

As I was preparing my dish on Saturday night for Sunday lunch, I realized I needed to double the recipe since there would be over fifty people. Whoa! My recipe looked to only feed about ten to twelve. I purchased a few extras on some of the ingredients since it was cheaper to purchase three items for ninety-nine cents instead of one for fifty-nine cents. But for the price of the eight-ounce Cool Whip, I decided only to purchase one.

INTRODUCTION

So, what did I do? I dumped another can of pineapple and the whole bag of marshmallows into the bowl. I prayed it would not matter that I had left out the extra Cool Whip and the pudding mix. I put it in the refrigerator to chill overnight.

I took my dish to the family Easter lunch, and several people said it was good. They went back for seconds and asked what was in it. Since I am the five-ingredients-or-less type of cook, I was able to tell them exactly what was in it.

I do not like using ingredients I cannot pronounce or that are not regular kitchen staples. In my opinion, if you have to purchase a seasoning specifically for one dish you are making one time… well, that's going to be a pass for me.

You know, in life, there are many times we feel like we do not have what it takes to accomplish a goal, be successful, or feel valuable. Our negative self-talk, lack of knowledge about the process, or fear of asking questions can hold us back. But I'd like to encourage you with the saying, "It's not where you start; it's where you finish."

Have you ever noticed children when they are learning to walk? They fall down and bounce right back up. It is like they do not know any better than to get back up. Some are so cute in the way they bounce back up. Usually, someone is videoing and clapping for the accomplishment of those first steps. Every Olympic runner starts out by taking those first steps. The first steps turn into short, slow distances, and eventually, they learn to run with endurance and speed. Our lives, Olympic runners or not, are similar.

How about when you were learning to ride a bike without the training wheels? You first had to learn balance and coordination. Oh my, and I am not Miss Grace by any means! Even then, I did not have negative self-talk or the mindset that I could not ride the bike. No—I had determination, focus, and an it-will-happen mindset, no matter what.

Think about a goal you are currently working on. Maybe you are still in the dreaming phase, or perhaps you are already in the midst of making it happen. How will you feel when the goal is complete? Who will be there with you on that stage? What will your family say when they are given the microphone? Who will be clapping for you?

I have overcome so many obstacles in my life, yet they have not stopped me from reaching multiple goals—yes, goals with an "s." Some I was aware of, and some I did not even know about. I pray you have more than one goal in your life. If not, I hope by the end of this book, you are dreaming big, beyond the skies.

In the human eye, some of my goals seemed impossible. I had people who were not cheering me on. After a few of these hard knocks, I realized that to have a testimony, you have to go through a test. Also, I felt like I had the wrong "ingredients," so to speak, to make these goals a reality. I felt like God had given me cabbage to make lemonade–because if He had given me lemons, it would have been too easy. *Okay, God… I will make the lemonade*; it is just that my process will have to be different. It will be the best lemonade around when I complete the process!

Who Is Tina Hunt?

Tina is a young American Indian lady who grew up in a small town in North Carolina called Huntersville. How fitting… Hunt and Huntersville, right? It was a small town, yet big enough to have privacy. I lived twenty-five minutes away from town. The area was considered the country, and our house was close to a dairy farm. I am honored to be an American Indian member of the Lumbee Tribe, the largest tribe East of the Mississippi.

In this once-small town of Huntersville, there was a single stop light in the center of town. We had one grocery store and a dentist. Why and how do I remember the dentist? Well, with only one option for a dentist, unfortunately, that dentist instilled in me the fear of having my teeth worked on. Oftentimes, growing up inside or near a small town, you just do not have a lot of choices for anything. We didn't have a computer to "Google" things, so we just took things for what they were.

My parents moved to the area when I was two years old. I can not say that I remember a lot about those early years, but I do remember our neighbors having older children with whom I was able to spend time with. Our neighbor's daughter, Julie, drove me to school. Since I am an only child, it was nice to have what I thought of as older siblings.

I would ride my bicycle to the community ball field we had near our home to play softball. I was not athletic, but it was fun, and I gave it my all. On my report cards from kindergarten through high school, I was consistent in receiving the letter "N" for unnecessary talking. Maybe I was thinking the "N" stood for "needs to talk more," right? Oh, I knew better, but I loved to talk no matter where I sat. I am sure none of you received such a mark. Anyway, on the ball team, I received my first trophy for the team clown. At the time, I had no idea my energetic, positive, and vibrant personality would be such a huge characteristic for me to succeed and survive in the years to come.

My parents were not what the world considers rich or wealthy. We lived humbly and comfortably on what we had. The one thing we were rich in was love, direction, and discipline. I had chores and curfews and did not question them. Driving the riding lawn mower was my first training in driving, and I was cutting the grass at the age of twelve. By the way, it was one of those clutch-style lawnmowers. The self-turn, one-button, push-button, and cruise-control, to name a few modern options, were not even available at the time. I went to Rockwell Baptist Church in a small town called Davidson, about thirty minutes away. I am so thankful for a strong Christian foundation in my early years of faith.

It was in this church that I accepted Jesus as my Savior at the age of thirteen. It was also in this church that I was able to use my musical talents and lessons learned in playing the piano and organ. One of my other neighbor's daughters, Sandy, started teaching me piano at the age of four. At the time, I thought the alphabet only went from A to G.

At my first piano recital, I did something to my big toe. Instead of the cute closed-toe shoes my mom had for me to wear, I wore cute sandals with my big toe wrapped in white gauze. That could have been a sign that I would be doing things a little differently in life.

Ingredients Needed

We have all heard of turning lemons into lemonade, but have you heard of turning cabbage into lemonade? For me, lemons to lemonade would be too easy. Plus, it would not have required the determination, growth, or mindset needed to keep going. "Cabbage" is the ingredient you have been dealt or have received by choices you have made. "Lemonade" is the road to success or the fulfillment you have of your dreams.

As we take this journey, you will see how the phrase "God gave me cabbage and told me to make lemonade—and I will make the lemonade" came about. Let's first discuss a few things needed to help you navigate this journey.

A few of the important ingredients that you will need in your kitchen are what I will refer to as your staples. First, you will need a positive attitude. Did you know that when you are positive, you draw people to you? Some of these people you attract usually have the same or similar characteristics as you, while others will be around to draw or drain from you. They want what you have but don't know how to get it. Some may even be jealous of you, so they want to be around to see you when you fall. Have healthy boundaries.

Secondly, your inner circle of friends is a staple in life. They will be your cheerleaders and your support when you are weak. In return, when one of them is struggling, you will be the one cheering or supporting them. This is huge as you will become like the five closest people you hang out with. Let me ask you something: after spending time with your friends, do you feel positive, negative, or the same? Think about that.

Your next "kitchen staple" is your mindset. Do you have the mindset that you can do whatever you set your mind to? Or do you give all the excuses as to why you can't? Remember how I talked about learning to walk? When you were a toddler, you had the bounce-back ability, and you just kept at it until you accomplished your goal of walking. Let's have a good supply of the mindset of determination in our kitchens. As you will read later, I have arthritis so bad I used to not even be able to open a gas tank. My mindset was (and is) that *I might have arthritis, but arthritis does not have me.* I was determined to keep driving and not fear running out of gas and not being able to pump the gas… I have a mindset of determination that I can and I will be able to open gas caps.

Are you a glass-half-full or a glass-half-empty kind of person? What is your perspective? Your perspective is a crucial staple in the recipe of life and attaining your goals. When you are looking for good, positive, and rewarding outcomes, that is usually what you get. Sometimes, there are blessings hidden in the battle. There is pain in natural childbirth, but the blessing of that precious child comes after the pain.

CABBAGE TO LEMONADE?

Last but certainly not least, you must have an "I can and I will" attitude. You will have obstacles in life. These obstacles could be from the choices you have made or it could be what you have been given. Sometimes, it's out of your control. Even still, you need to make this lemonade with the cabbage you have. You can turn these obstacles into opportunities! When you overcome obstacles, you build strength and character. Are you a victim or a victor? A victim sees obstacles, while a victor sees opportunities.

> *A victim sees obstacles, while a victor sees opportunities.*

When you have all the staple ingredients of a positive attitude, a solid circle of friends, the right mindset, determination, the right perspective, and the "I can and I will" attitude, you will be unstoppable and will better yourself and those around you.

Now, let me share some of the steps of my personal journey through my health issues and how these ingredients came into play.

Cabbage Number One - The Diagnosis

My first cabbage thrown into my cart was in February 1984, my senior year of high school. I was diagnosed with Systemic Lupus Erythematosus (SLE) or Lupus. *What in the world is that?!* At that time, there was no internet to Google it. On the first of February, I went to my pediatrician to have my physical for college; I wasn't quite eighteen yet. Back then, a physical was required to attend the medical college I was planning to attend. This physical said everything was fine.

Well, two weeks later, I noticed fluid buildup on my knees. Remember, I am not athletic. I only played softball for the community, and they allowed *anyone* to play. Being the self-proclaimed doctor that I am, I self-diagnosed myself to drink more water and assured myself that it would flush out. My next thought was, "Let me go to the doctor and get the fluid drained off." It was my senior year, and I had stuff to do.

Well, that visit did not go as I had planned. The doctor wanted to do all kinds of blood work. The results came back showing I had Lupus. Those results lead to a kidney biopsy to confirm my

CABBAGE NUMBER ONE – THE DIAGNOSIS

diagnosis. Boy, had I missed the target on this one! Not only that, but I had just lost control of my plans for the future.

Systemic Lupus Erythematosus (SLE), or Lupus, is an auto-immune condition in which the body's immune system mistakenly attacks healthy tissue in many parts of the body. Of course, symptoms vary, but for me, the key indicator was the red rash across my face. It looked like a butterfly. I knew I needed to contact the doctor when this happened. Also, my particular type of Lupus could travel to other systems in my body. I am so blessed that mine was diagnosed early and accurately. This condition is so often misdiagnosed, even today. Let me say here: listen to your body. When something is not right, go get it checked out.

My momma came to the school to share the news with me in person. I was to go get my books and personal belongings from class, then meet her at home before heading to the hospital. Immediately, my plans were altered. You see, this was the weekend of our high school boys basketball championship. Suddenly, I was not going to be able to go because I would be in the hospital that weekend. Needless to say, I was not a happy teenager. Well, while crying and walking back to class, I saw Richard, a classmate. He asked what was wrong, and I shared the news with him. He hugged my neck and said it would be okay. He would pray and share with my classmates.

Thankfully, my friends came to the hospital to visit before the game. Again, I was more upset about missing the game than I was about the actual diagnosis. Let me add that not only did we not have cell phones, but my graduating class was over 400 students.

When my friends arrived, my mother went down to the cafeteria. She knew how upset I was, and she knew being with my friends would be good medicine. So, my friends and I came up with a brilliant idea for me to be included in the basketball festivities. We were smart seniors about to graduate high school–you know, we knew everything. The idea was we would play basketball in my room. I would roll the brown paper towels into a ball and throw them into the trash can from my bed. They would move the trash can around to different people. There were eight of us in the room.

Shortly into our clever game, a nurse came in after hearing the commotion. She did not like basketball, I guess, because she made us stop playing, and my friends had to leave. When my momma came back, she asked how I enjoyed my visit with my friends and if they left earlier than expected. I told her I did enjoy them, but the nurse did not like it when we started playing basketball. My mom gave me a puzzled look and asked, "How did y'all play basketball?" I shared our brilliant basketball idea with her. Then she asked me if we got loud. I replied sheepishly, "Kind of..." I guess I had forgotten briefly I was in the hospital.

Well, the month of May rolled around, and it was time to go to Disney World in Florida to sing with the school choir. My family did not travel out of state a lot, so I was excited to be going to Disney World. However, with my new diagnosis and current medications, I was not supposed to be in the sun very much... Now, how can you go to Disney and not be in the sun?

My parents knew the chaperones who were going and knew they would take good care of me like their own child. So, after going through a lot more obstacles and planning than my classmates, I was off to Disney. I *needed* this fun trip.

CABBAGE NUMBER ONE – THE DIAGNOSIS

This is when my cabbage-to-lemonade journey began. I had not finished high school, and my future plans were changing all around me. This is not how I had pictured my life to be! You see, I was saved. I had accepted Jesus into my heart at the age of thirteen. I used my talents to play the piano and organ at my church. I followed and lived for Him daily.

I finished my senior year of high school with this new health condition called Lupus that no one had ever heard of (this was before the internet, of course). I was so blessed to have supportive friends and their parents who helped me and my parents with this diagnosis. It is super important who you have in your circle of friends. I had taken the cabbage that I was given in February and fought through to make the first jug of lemonade by graduating high school, with God as the guide for it all.

Cabbage Number Two – College Opportunities with Determination

I graduated high school in June 1984, and on July 9, 1984, I started college, blessed with a private scholarship donor. You see, a four-year college was not my groove, even before the Lupus diagnosis. I was more like, "Hey, let me take the classes I need and keep it moving. I've got things to do!" Have you ever made plans that did not go as you had planned? If so, how did you handle that?

King's College in Charlotte, NC, offered the degree I was interested in as a Medical Office Assistant (MOA). It was a two-year program crammed into eight-and-a-half months. Yes, I said *crammed*, not *condensed*. The schedule was five days a week, six hours a day, dressed in a nursing uniform. It was truly getting me ready for the real world.

This was the first of many obstacles—or what I like to call opportunities. As I stated earlier, perspective is an important staple ingredient. I was in college for two weeks when I had my first Lupus flare-up. Two weeks! This flare-up was one big head of cabbage—I mean a *big one*!

CABBAGE NUMBER TWO – COLLEGE OPPORTUNITIES WITH DETERMINATION

The flare-up resulted in me being in the hospital for several days. As only God would have it, the hospital was right next door to the college. So, I requested my classes be recorded and brought to me with my homework assignments. Recorded as in, on a tape recorder; there was no such thing as a cell phone recorder back then!

Yes, I was a little slow, but I did not get behind. I had to work differently from the other students while still going after the same goal. Not only did I have to work differently, but I also had to work harder and longer. My weekends were spent doing homework. I went to church on Sunday morning, but other than that, the rest of the weekend was all homework.

I wish I could say the hospital stay was only a one-time thing, but another flare-up hit me in mid-September. As this was not my first time, we did the same thing as before. Thankfully, this was my last hospital trip while in college. I encountered numerous chances to gain important life lessons while simultaneously battling an illness and earning my college degree in Medical Office Assistant with cum laude honors.

One important lesson I learned during a doctor's visit. I had been struggling with the reason and purpose of my being diagnosed with Lupus. I was asking God, "*Why me?*" I know that different people have different views on this type of question, but I'll give you my take. You see, God knows my heart. He knew I was struggling. I talk to Him just like I talk to people. I wasn't questioning God, but I just couldn't understand the purpose at this time in my life.

As I was in the waiting area at one of my doctor visits, I saw an older gentleman come in with an oxygen tube around his nose, pulling an oxygen tank behind him, yes, pulling! Back then, they were big, but they did have wheels so you could roll them. As I watched this man get around with all his equipment, God spoke to me and said, *It could be worse, Tina. You can handle what I have given you because I am with you.* That was all I needed to carry on and give God glory in and through it all. It's not always easy, but I appreciate the reminders, and I still remember the man with the oxygen tank.

In March of 1985, I graduated on the honor roll. Yes, the honor roll! Graduating under so many obstacles (or, as I call them, opportunities) was one thing. But being on the honor roll was a different kind of accomplishment. That was lemonade in a crystal glass! I remember, to this day, a lady in my class being upset because she did not see how I made the honor roll with me being in the hospital! Well… my answer to her is that I was focused and determined. And, maybe I had no other option but to finish and finish well. Failure was not an option for me!

I graduated on a Friday and started working full-time the following Monday. The office where I did my internship even created a job for me. I was so thankful that I did not have to go through the process of searching for a job. Jehovah-Jireh, my God, provided. You know, He is good like that.

Graduation day highlights included me being so swollen from the steroids I was on for Lupus that I could not bend over to tie my nursing shoes. On this particular day, it felt like a tractor-trailer truck had just unloaded a hundred pallets of cabbage onto my body. My mother had to help me with so many things, including getting dressed that day.

I also learned that day at the graduation reception that the college and professors had wanted me to quit. They felt it would be best if I came back the next year. In their minds, there was no way I would pass and keep up with being in the hospital. With Lupus being a new diagnosis to me, I was learning about all the things that were popping up. Talk about a day of mixed emotions! From using every bit of energy, I had to get dressed in my nursing uniform (which included pantyhose; if you are under 30, you can Google it. Ha!) to receiving my diploma to being told my professors had wanted me to drop out; the day of my college graduation was a rollercoaster! I don't like rollercoasters, even in real life!

Thankfully, my parents and doctors said, "No." They knew I could and would no matter the opportunities (obstacles). I worked with what I had, and I knew that I could do it. This led to another glass of lemonade to enjoy.

There are a couple of lessons here:

1. Make sure those making decisions for you know you and have your best interest at hand.

2. What you tell yourself or allow others to speak over you could lift you up or pull you down. Guard your heart and mind.

Cabbage Number Three – The Fall with "I Can" and "I Will"

In 1986, two years later, the Lupus went from my kidneys to my joints. Remember I told you my Lupus could go from system to system? Yet again, another load of cabbage. How could I be so blessed to have the Lupus that wants to travel? So, on top of Lupus, I also had Rheumatoid Arthritis (RA) at the young age of twenty. Before the internet, I was unable to research or connect with any other young people for support.

The support groups I attended were all adults. They didn't understand my struggles as a young person with such a disease. Believe it or not, I didn't talk much during the meetings. Now, if that wasn't bad enough, the conversations that surrounded me were all depressing and negative. The discussions these group members had were all about the problems they encountered with RA, and they didn't end with how to overcome them. I could only handle attending these meetings for a few months before I finally asked my parents and doctors if I could stop going. They agreed, and I was thankful.

This was a tough period of time as people would ask why my fingers were crooked; trying to explain arthritis was hard. What I

CABBAGE NUMBER THREE – THE FALL WITH "I CAN" AND "I WILL"

started saying and still say to this day is, "God thought my fingers should be crooked." Everyone seemed to be okay with that answer, from the young to the old. A toast with lemonade, please!

April 2, 1990, I had been on steroids for six years, and yet another hundred pallets of cabbage came my way. What you may or may not know about steroids is that there is a strong chance of gaining weight, especially in the beginning. The medication itself will bloat you. Then, on top of that, it makes you want to eat. So, I was eating half a gallon of ice cream, bananas, and vanilla wafers before bed, every night. Yes, I had a good breakfast, lunch, and dinner, along with snacks. Those were just my bedtime snacks!

I am known as someone who plans ahead, and I was expected to be a bridesmaid in a wedding in June, just two months away. To combat the weight gain, I started walking in the evenings after work, with the goal of being at my target weight before the wedding. Now, we are not even going to talk about how much I needed to lose. There are some things that you just do not need to know.

One night, while at a good friend's house, after walking two miles, we noticed a storm coming, so I got my things to go home. As I walked down the steps, my knees gave out, and I fell. My head barely missed the brick steps. I was so thankful for the position of the fall, as it could have been worse.

Due to the embarrassment and hoping none of the neighborhood teenagers saw me, I tried to get back up but found out later that it was a big mistake. In the fall, I pulled muscles, tendons, and more. By now, everyone in the neighborhood, including my friend and her husband, were surrounding me. As everyone was trying to figure out what to do and how to do it, I asked that someone check my car windows because they were down and the rain was coming. Priorities: I had a new car.

It was obvious I could not stand up. I didn't feel the need for an ambulance (looking back, that is what we should have done). So, the next best thing was to pick me up and put me in an outdoor lounge chair to get me to the car for transport to the ER. As one of the guys stated, "Tina, this would be easier if you did not weigh so much." My reply was, "Why do you think I was walking?" Of course, everyone was laughing now. We needed some humor at this point!

Thank God for station wagon cars because that is how they got me safely into the car! Some people helped from the back of the car, pulling me from the back across the seat and keeping my legs straight. Again, this was before phone videos, or this surely would have made it to *America's Funniest Home Videos*. We would have over a trillion views for sure, and it would still be viewed some thirty-plus years later at the writing of this book.

By now, we had called my parents. It was the night of the March Madness Championship basketball game, and my dad thought we were making a joke on him. Unfortunately for him, it wasn't, and my parents met us at the small local hospital emergency room. We quickly realized I was too much of a complicated case, and I needed to go to the larger hospital in Charlotte. I called my employer, and they, too, thought it was a late April Fool's joke. This hospital did get my legs splinted, but I still could not stand up. I came home to basically wait to go to the hospital ER in Charlotte the next morning. I forgot to mention that there was no pain during all of this, which is remarkable. The local hospital did give me something in case I needed anything for pain overnight, however.

Upon arrival at the Charlotte ER and several x-rays later, it was confirmed my kneecaps had come off in both knees, which resulted in both knees needing surgery. The surgeon was confident he could do the surgery and no screws or plates would be needed, unlike the other hospital, which wanted to put a bunch of metal in me. It would be one surgery for both knees at the same time, with one recovery. I could get excited about that! At the same time, I did not know what to expect.

As they began the surgery to put the kneecaps back on, it was discovered that my tendon had come loose, too. Remember, I told you I tried to get up after I fell. This was the result of the knee caps coming off and tendons loose. Due to the tendon now needing to be repaired, they had to cut up and down like the letter "I." So, you ask, "What is the significance of that?" My knee scars spell the word "IT." Yes, one knee has an "I"; the other knee has a "T." My cousins nicknamed me "Cousin It." Laughter is good for the soul. Proverbs 17:22 says, "A merry heart doeth good like a medicine; But a broken spirit drieth the bones" (KJV).

For me personally, I am thankful I only had to have one surgery and one recovery. It was a long recovery, so I cannot imagine having to do it twice! Another key factor was that I had the support to get through it, as you will read about later.

I was in the hospital for a week, learning how to use bedpans and pulling on the overhead bed rails. Now, I will be honest and say this was not an easy task, but one I had to master and had no other choice. Plus, to come home, I had to have a ramp built to enter my house, as well as a hospital bed with overhead rails, a bedside table, etc. You know, all things hospital.

Cabbage Number Four - Will I Ever Walk Again?

I remember coming home seated on the floor of our van. Because my legs were in straight splints, there was no bending of the knees. Pulling up to my home, seeing the ramp, and knowing my house was now going to look like a hospital, I cried. The thought crossed my mind, *Would I, could I, walk again?* The ramp was and is special in that my uncles and close friends put it up, and quickly at that. It was sturdy and sufficient. The ramp is still up as I'm writing this, and it has come in handy over the years.

Not knowing my parents had been told by the doctors that I would not walk again, I was determined to walk. And guess what? It was a long process, but I did it. Once again, my parents stood up for me behind the scenes, which bolstered my determination to succeed and walk.

Let me insert here that my parents had been through a lot learning about this Lupus thing. The lack of support from professionals was astounding. At every turn, they were told, "Your daughter can not do this, or your daughter can not do that." Both of my parents worked full-time jobs. As a family, we were blessed with a blood-kin family and our church family. Without this, it would have been impossible. This was also before home health agencies came to your home.

When I called the couple to say I could not be at their wedding in June, the groom replied, "You will be at our wedding, even if you are on a gurney." Not only was I able to attend the wedding, but I was included in all the pre-wedding activities, from the bridesmaid luncheon to getting my dyed purple shoes, just like all the other bridesmaids. It was time-consuming because they had to bring me my shoes first to make sure they fit. Then, they took them back to dye.

One cool thing I remember about the luncheon was seeing my first-ever cell phone. *Wow!* It was like carrying another purse! The phone was big and in a bag. I just kept thinking, *Kristi's aunt is rich.* Do you remember seeing your first cell phone? That question is for the more mature folks reading now. For the younger folks, Google that one. You will get a good laugh.

The recovery was a long and painful process. It took a village of family, friends, neighbors, and church family, young and old, to assist in my recovery process. Therapy did not start until May because I had to give enough time for healing before any bending or weight-bearing could begin. When you don't use your muscles, you lose your strength. To wake them up, they used shock electrodes. Well, glory, it woke them up all right– with a little pain.

Since I was somewhat limited in my energy and mobility, it took me a week to get ready for the wedding, but I was wedding-ready come the wedding day. I still carried out my bridesmaid duties. I walked in with a walker from the side of the church and went out in a wheelchair. I went to the reception in my wheelchair. I'm still known, thirty-plus years later, as the girl at Neal and Kristi's wedding who was in a wheelchair. Being in a wheelchair and having a walker was just another opportunity for me to overcome. This lemonade was served and drank out of a crystal glass.

Oh, how did I get to therapy? I sat on the floor of the van. In the beginning, it would take two people to get me to therapy. At first, it was my mom and another person, as my dad had to go back to work. Then, after about three months, my mom had to go back to work. My aunt moved in with us to help while my parents worked.

On one trip, I specifically remember two of the young teenage boys from my church taking me to therapy. I told you, young and old, they all were a part of my recovery. The boys suggested that it would be a good idea for us to go hunting since it was hunting season. They believed that spending time outdoors would be good for me. While we didn't end up hunting, we did drive down a dirt road in search of deer. Memories!

It took a year for me to be able to drive again, but I felt ready to return to work. I was bored staying in the house. My mom said I could spot every cobweb and dust spot. So, after five months, Ms. Dessie would come pick me up and drive me to work. I would wheelchair into the office two or three days a week for three to four hours a day to build my strength and stamina.

Remember I mentioned playing the organ at church? My mindset was that my knees were messed up, but not my hands. The church youth would wheel me back and forth to the organ. Legs still in straight splints, I would turn to the side and play that organ. The youth thought it was the coolest thing in the world.

Plus, most of the youth were there the night I fell. They had been on this journey with me from the beginning.

This one particular Sunday was Mike's turn to wheel me back from the organ. Because of my legs being straight out, we would have to make wide turns. We came down the aisle, and the preacher was now at the pulpit to start the sermon. Mike made the turn with the wheelchair; however, he did not have enough clearance. This loud noise... BAM! Everyone looked to see if I had fallen out of the wheelchair. Mike had hit the pew with my wheelchair so hard it took a chunk out of the pew. Everyone was relieved I was not lying on the floor. Do you know how hard it is not to laugh in church? This was one of those times. We had to hold the laughs till after church.

In the fall of this same year, I am attending my cousin Melanie's outdoor wedding. The venue was her parent's backyard. Naturally, it was not wheelchair accessible or laid out the best. However, because I was in a wheelchair, I was seated close to the front and close to the bride and groom. The ceremony began, and Melanie, the bride, had forgotten her flowers. She looked at me and said, "Go get the flowers out of the refrigerator." I looked at her and pointed to my legs, which were straight out in the wheelchair with braces on. We still laugh about that today. She did go and get her own flowers.

I am forever grateful for those who supported me during this process, as it truly took a village and then some. Be careful and wise about who you hang out with.

You must have faith. Matthew 13:31-32 says we are to have faith like the size of a mustard seed. Though it is the smallest of all seeds, yet when it grows, it is the largest of garden plants and becomes a tree. The birds come and perch in its branches.

Give Up, Give In, or Give It Your All

Have you ever been between a rock and a hard place, trying to decide if you should continue on or just give up? First of all, giving up is like quitting, and quitters never win. Sometimes, right about the time you are ready to throw in the towel, the next step, or the next turn, is just what you were waiting for. Sometimes, you just have to say, *I will try one more time*. That one more ounce of effort is just what you need to make the difference. You now see the light at the end of the tunnel. Remember, the rainbow most of the time comes after the storm.

You see, most would have given up by now with all I had been through. Well, as I said earlier, I did not know any better but to keep pressing forward. Philippians 3:14 says, "I press toward the mark for the prize of the high calling of God in Christ Jesus" (KJV).

One thing I am not is athletic, especially as a runner, but let's look at a runner for an example anyway. A runner starts the race with the full intent to win. He is running to the finish line. He wants the gold medal and to stand on the top box. Some have seen in their minds the finish line even before the day of the race.

Quitting, getting distracted, or negative self-talk is not an option. In the runner's mind, winning and finishing are all he knows.

Giving up is like quitting, and quitters never win.

Why in life do we get so distracted and allow negative self-talk to stop us? Whether it is in our dreams or everyday life, we must keep going strong. It's important to have goal posters or tracking sheets as visual reminders of your progress. You know, a tracked number increases over time. Be clear, be focused, and be passionate about your why. Who is attached to your goal, and what is the impact it will have when it is complete?

Check your mindset when others say, "It can't be done." You show them how to and make it look simple. You are that duck that looks so calm above the water, but underneath, you are paddling away. Do not focus on the obstacles. Instead, turn them into opportunities for success. Your success depends on where you focus your time and energy.

During this time, life did not get easier or simpler. I still had cabbage given to me. I'd like to share several of these loads of cabbage with you just to give you an idea of the obstacles – *opportunities* – that came my way.

My first example of another head of cabbage was the ruptured ulcer that took forever to find. If anyone simply touched the bed on which I laid, I hurt. I was begging for them to cut me open so the doctor could find the problem. They finally did the test that showed a ruptured ulcer, and off to surgery I went. There was no prep—we were immediately off and rolling. Because it was an internal issue, it was best that it healed from the inside out. My mom and I had to learn how to pack and change the bandages ourselves.

Another head of cabbage I was given was on a lunch date at Fuddruckers after church with a cute guy. I fell on the slick floor, and by now, I had learned not to try and get up. So I had to ask him to call 911. Because we had not discussed my health challenges, he did not realize how fragile my bones were. The fall resulted in a dislocated hip, but as you know by now, I was not defined by this. A little side note: I did feel like Cinderella for a moment as my shoe came off in the fall. It was left at the restaurant, and when this cute guy I had been on a date with arrived to check on me at the hospital, he brought me my shoe.

I also had to have my gallbladder removed. The doctor was hopeful of being able to remove it laparoscopically if everything was in place as it should be. I replied, "Well, you were the last one in there, so it should be how you left it!" I was blessed by my friend Charlotte, a licensed massage therapist, who gave me a special alignment massage. That was the best massage ever! It worked to align my internal organs, and I was able to have the same-day laparoscopic surgery and come home. My doctor was shocked when I told him afterward what I had done.

For eighteen months, I was taking chemotherapy because my doctors thought it would help put my Lupus in remission or possibly even cure it. Thankfully, I only had treatments every three months, but I dreaded the after-effects. Not only that, I was also scared of the whole process of chemotherapy. I made sure the nurses didn't miss anything in the process, a copy of the doctor's orders in hand. I would check everything off as they put the drug in the IV machine. The process was a minimum of four hours, though sometimes it went for up to six hours. Due to the duration of this process, I requested calming medicine. Sometimes, when it was a long morning into lunchtime, you and whoever was with you received a box lunch. The "fun" part was coming home and feeling miserable. There was no relief until I threw up. Then I felt so much better.

I have had two surgeries on my right hand to clean out arthritis. Since I am right-handed, we will start with that one. A year post-surgery, my hand was no better than before. The surgeon did not understand why my hand function did not get better. The same surgeon said, "I guess I should have put artificial knuckles in." So, I let him go back in to put the artificial knuckles in my hand. It helped a little, but nothing major. He then wanted to do the left hand. Well, I'm not crazy! Two surgeries on the right hand, some better, but no significant change? I told him, "I will learn to live with the arthritis in my left hand as it is."

During my hand surgery recovery, one of my cousins, Patsy, thought I deserved a trip to the beach. Two surgeries in less than two years—that is a lot! So off to the beach we went! My mom, Patsy, her husband, her son, and myself all went on this trip. I knew anytime I was in water, I would need to wrap my hand, but I didn't mind; I was ready for some fun!

What is one of the first trips you make when you arrive at the beach for a few days? To the grocery store, of course! We headed to the store to stock up on all the fun, unhealthy beach snacks. This was before Walmart was everywhere, so Piggly Wiggly... here we come! At the beach grocery stores, they sell more than food. They also have floats, chairs, surfboards, and small boat floats, just to name a few things. They sold all of the items that would help make your trip more enjoyable… and cause you to spend more money.

Along with our food, we purchased one of the small boat floats. We had so much fun with it the first day. That evening, we discussed getting another one.

On the second day, early in the morning, we went back to Piggly Wiggly to get another $19.99 boat float. We got the float ready for the water and left our towels on the beach with my mom in her chair. At this point, we were like four kids on Christmas morning. Off into the water with these two floats! This way, all four of us could float beside each other. My cousin, her husband, son, and I got out onto the water with our two Piggly Wiggly boat floats. I wish I could say we didn't fall out, but we did.

You ask, what is so special about three grown adults and a teenager at the beach with two Piggly Wiggly $19.99 boat floats? I hope you are ready for this.

1. None of us could swim.

2. My right hand was wrapped in a towel taped to my wrist and "waterproofed," with two or three plastic Piggly Wiggly bags over the towel taped above the wrist.

3. When one of us would fall out, the others would start laughing.

4. When I fell out, my right hand would instantly go up in the air above the water, and they would help me with my one good hand to get back in the boat.

5. The lifeguard had to call us back close to shore a couple of times for being too far out.

6. We would wave to my mom every once in a while, and she would wave back.

Now, when we did get out of the water with our boat floats, we looked for Momma. We had gone two miles away from her. Where she was seated is where we got in the water. *What?* We had drifted that far?! When we got to her, she said she could keep track of us by watching me raise my hand when I fell out of the boat. She said, "I sat here and prayed." I sure am thankful for a praying momma! Have you ever heard the saying, "God looks after babies and fools, and you ain't no baby?" That was us, for sure.

Let's talk about drifting here for a minute. Have you ever gotten in a situation and asked, *How did I get here?* Well, friend, you drifted. You didn't mean to get so far away. However, it became consistent and constant without you knowing. It felt good and was fun. We drift by neglecting our focus, location, or purpose. Sometimes, we follow the wrong crowd–and they are "bad," and you are "good" or vice-versa. We just lost track of our location. I am thankful for a praying momma on the sidelines, a physical lifeguard, and God

We drift by neglecting our focus, location, or purpose.

who was watching over us. This deserves a toast of lemonade on the beach at sunset. Cheers!

I want you to realize here that you must not give up, but you can and must go on. It may not be easy, but I can tell you it will be worth it. You see, to have a testimony, you must go through a test. I am so blessed to share my tests and testimonies with you in this book.

Let us continue on because I have more testimonies to share as I share the good, the bad, the ugly, and the beautiful, along with lots of laughs.

If we look at the story of Joseph in the Bible in Genesis chapter 39, it is obvious that he had two choices to make: he could give up, or he could continue on. Joseph's profile is that of a leadership position. Dreams can contain surprises that can be discouraging. However, because things don't go as planned, there is no reason to give up; you simply just take the detour. You usually throw the basketball more times than you get it in the net, right? No matter where Joseph was, he realized the Lord was with him, and he didn't waver.

Genesis 39:21 reminds us that "The Lord was with him; he showed him kindness and granted him favor in the eyes of the prison warden" (NIV).

Cabbage Number Five - Shocked and Scared

In 2003, I started having frequent Lupus flare-ups. The flares would take me out of commission for several days. In April 2004, I was told I would have to quit my job. By this point, I had been served thousands of pallets of cabbage. I loved being a Medical Office Assistant. However, there was too much wear and tear on my body. On my last day, I worked fourteen hours. This obstacle/opportunity was a hard one, and to this day, I am still in the process of turning it into lemonade.

In 2008, I was told my kidney function was at twenty percent. Therefore, I needed to go on the kidney transplant list. Well, glory! This news was a shock as I felt fine. Where did this load of cabbage come from?

When I was given this news, I was shocked and scared. A kidney transplant is a major and serious surgery. At that time, I did not know anyone who had undergone a kidney transplant. My emotions and feelings were all over the place. It is hard to describe and explain. I had tons of questions, yet I was not sure how or what to ask.

CABBAGE NUMBER FIVE - SHOCKED AND SCARED

I remember writing down a lot of medical questions for the doctors. I did a lot of praying and asked many of my friends for prayer. I knew that in order to tackle this load of cabbage, I needed backup and reinforcement. At my doctor's visits, I would have a page of questions written down. In person at the appointment, one written question would lead to another question I had not written down. I changed my eating lifestyle by giving up a Route 44 Sonic strawberry limeade two to three times a week. A year later, I was off the transplant list.

In March of 2010, I had to go back on the transplant list. This time, I started doing fundraisers and looking for a donor. Do you know what it is like asking people for their kidneys? There was no shame in my game; I did *not* want to go on dialysis.

So, I came up with a game plan. I would go to Lumbee Homecoming in Pembroke, NC, to set up a tent to educate people on how to become an organ donor. I also asked if anyone would be willing to donate a kidney for me. Now, Lumbee Homecoming, on average, brings in about 50,000 attendees. Surely, I could find one match. I also rode around on a golf cart with a sign asking for a kidney. So, for three days, I stood at my booth asking for a donor. At the end of the three days, I had ten potential living donors and lots of people who said they would pray. I was excited for both.

I came back to Charlotte and met with my transplant coordinator. At the appointment, she asked how it went, and I gave her the forms from the ten potential donors. At that point, they reviewed them all and chose one to start the testing process. In the first report I received, one of my potential donors was a perfect match. Well, glory, hallelujah! However, three or four months into their testing resulted in this person not being a match, after all. It was disappointing and an emotional roller coaster ride. But as you will read, you will see God had something better for me.

In June of 2011, my mother fell at the age of 77 years young at the time. Her fall resulted in her having knee surgery. At that time, things shifted in my life forever. Cabbage was one thing for me, but cabbage for my mother was totally different.

I became her full-time caregiver. Everything was on me being the only child. My dad would just agree to my decisions. To this day, I have no regrets about my life being altered to care for my mother. Deuteronomy 5:16 says, "Honour thy father and thy mother, as the LORD your God has commanded thee, in the land which the Lord thy God giveth thee, so that your days may be prolonged and that it may go well for you on the land which the LORD your God is giving you" (KJV).

My mother first served as my parent, which fostered a strong relationship and respect for her and later resulted in us being best friends. We did many things together, like shopping, going on day trips, etc. It is a friendship I will always cherish. There is nothing like a mother's love.

Throughout her healing process, numerous adjustments took place. We arranged for home health services to be provided in the house, ensuring that visits were coordinated to avoid scheduling conflicts that could impact insurance coverage. We got things done. Actually, I learned a lot of organizational and planning skills during this time. The home health people even took some of my ideas and shared them with other patients.

The Call

In April of 2012, I felt like I had never felt before. The feeling told me I would be getting my kidney this summer. Yet because no one was being tested as my donor, I was not confident of my discernment at the time. Regardless, that feeling lingered. Therefore, I did not share this with anyone. Have you ever heard from God, but you did not believe it? It was just too good to be true.

I received a call at four o'clock in the afternoon on Thursday, June 21, 2012, and was told I was fourth on the list for a "perfect match" kidney. My feelings were a mix of shock and anxiety–but not surprise. *Oh my, it is time to start making some lemonade!* After the call, I shared the news with my parents and best friend. She then called others that we knew to join us for an evening of prayer.

This group was known as "The Divas," a group of my high school friends that had monthly lunches, etc. At prayer time, I was reminded of my request that I had prayed for no dialysis and a perfect match. God heard and answered my prayer. After the evening prayer, I had peace and calmness. I came home, paid bills, and packed my clothes. God knew I was a planner, for He created

THE CALL

me. He knew I needed a notice. You usually receive a call, and you have about an hour or two to get to the hospital.

On Friday morning, June 22, 2012, at about 8:30 AM, I called my transplant coordinator to let her know that if it was God's will, I was ready. She was partly shocked, but then again, not, for she knew my relationship with the Lord.

At lunch, I met with the rest of the Diva group for prayer. I had been instructed to stay near my phone, so the transplant center called often to make sure I was following orders. As I was in the waiting period, I kept myself busy. After lunch, I went to a hair salon.

I walked into a salon close to my house, having never been there before. They asked how they could help me. I replied, "I am waiting for a call to get a kidney, and I need a good hair wash with a deep conditioner as I will not be able to wash my hair for a few weeks." To which they replied, "Sure, we will be right with you." The stylist who provided my care asked more questions. So, I filled her in on everything. I received my hair treatment, and I went home to wait.

As I was sitting at my desk doing some last-minute things, which included eating banana pudding, I received *the call* at 4:30 PM that same Friday. The doctor himself called me and asked a few medical questions. He followed with, "How long will it take you to get to the hospital?" He stated that if everything continued to stay on track, I would be receiving a kidney.

I arrived at the hospital at about 6 PM with my parents and my uncle Clinton. My parents and my uncle Clinton were with me for every appointment, including lab work. As I checked into the hospital, they confirmed my reason for me being there. A young guy with transport got me a wheelchair. I said, "I'm good. I can walk." He looked at my papers again, confused. I repeated, "Yes, I'm here for a kidney transplant, but I can walk." He was shocked. I must say I was looking good, hair and all.

One of the funniest things upon arrival in the room was that the nurse asked me to shower with the betadine soap. I replied, "What?! I just paid good money to get my hair done since I would not be able to wash it for a couple of weeks!" We compromised that I would shower from my neck down without getting my hair wet.

There was a lot of prep work that Friday night, and the transplant was scheduled for Saturday, June 23, 2012. I remained calm and stayed busy. How did I stay busy? I stayed on the phone talking with family and friends. There was no time to let my mind think. Even though I took something to relax, I chose to stay busy and active. I was walking the halls at 11 PM talking on the phone. I was so blessed with friends who helped me to stay busy.

I talked with friends until midnight, and my mother spent the night with me. Neither one of us slept much that night with all the anticipation that was to come. I had prayed for this for over four years, and the time had finally come. In the transplant world, four years was not a long time, but it felt like an eternity to me.

Saturday, June 23, 2012, had finally arrived, and family and friends started arriving in my room at about 5:30 AM for the 6:00 AM surgery. The time given for surgery was 6 AM, but you know how things change in the hospital world. My cousin Sarah and

THE CALL

her husband, Duane, who came in from out of town, wore pajamas since they left home at 2:00 AM. Upon arrival at the hospital, they changed in the parking deck. Smiling really big as they entered my room, they shared about traveling in their pj's. They stated no one saw them change clothes since it was an empty parking deck. We started smiling really big, talking about the cameras in the parking deck, and at this point, we knew lots of people around the hospital were laughing.

At 6:45 AM, the nurse came into my room and said, "It is official; the kidney is yours, and it is a perfect match. Transport will come to get you at 10 AM." Can you say, *Praise the Lord?* I think now would be a good time for a glass of lemonade! My room was filling up with family and friends, and cell phones were ringing as people checked in. There was more testing prior to the surgery, but we were getting closer to show time.

At 9:55 AM, transport came to my room to pick me up, which was now full of family and friends. As I went down the elevator with not one but two full elevators of family and friends, I had God's strength, a strong support system, and a feeling of calm and peace.

Entering the operating room, I saw the surgeon prepping my "new" kidney. I stated, "If y'all would have let me bring my phone in, I could have taken a picture of my kidney." That was the last thing I remember before they put the mask on me and put me to sleep. You see, they had given me medicine earlier in the morning that was supposed to make me a little sleepy. Mind over matter, I was having a party in my head. My Scripture verse for the kidney transplant was Psalm 30:2, which says, "O LORD my God, I cried to You for help, and You healed me" (KJV).

Every day in the hospital, I was blessed with support from family and friends. Medical staff said whenever they came into my room, it was like a party with so many people, flowers, cards, and balloons. I replied, "I told you that from the beginning. I have a lot of friends." Something I do not take for granted is my circle of friends.

I had no surgical complications, so I was discharged the following Saturday, June 30, 2012. Transport rushed me out on that day, but I had to remind them that I was a transplant recipient just a week earlier, so recovery had only been a week. Because I had been in the hospital preoccupied with getting a kidney and oblivious to the outside world, they shared with me the temperature outside was expected to reach over 100 degrees that day, and it could be a shock to my body in itself. I said okay, and we rushed to the car. Would you join me in a toast of lemonade?

During my recovery, I thought it would be appropriate to name my kidney. So, I reached out to my high school classmates to help me name it. We are a close group, and even to this day, we have a reunion every five years. We pray and support one another as needed. One classmate suggested Gloria as my kidney's name. We knew the donor was a female, and I am always saying, "Well, glory!" Another classmate suggested the name Blessing because I was a blessing to others. So, my kidney's official name became Gloria Blessing.

We even made a birth certificate for my kidney, including surgery date, time, etc. I put these in all of my thank-you notes. My kidney transplant experience was truly something special, as it took a village.

Let me share about my organ donor. I have not met the family since I wrote this book. She died from the results of a gunshot wound. Have you heard the saying, "What the devil meant for evil, God can work it out for good?"

Genesis 50:19-21 reads, "But Joseph said to them, "Don't be afraid. Am I in the place of God? You intended to harm me, but God intended it for good to accomplish what is now being done: the saving of many lives. So then, don't be afraid. I will provide for you and your children." And he reassured them and spoke kindly to them" (NIV).

I think and pray for her family often. Please look for more information about becoming an organ donor at the end of the book.

Cabbage Number Six - Where Did This Cabbage Come From?

On Friday, May 31, 2014, I attended an 80's musical with my best friend and her husband. It was great, and we had a blast. The next morning, I woke up with a 100-plus fever and didn't feel right. Of course, it was a Saturday, so I called my kidney doctors. They told me to come to the emergency room and they would meet me there.

Well, you know the chaos of an emergency room on the weekend, and this hospital is a trauma hospital to top it off. At each station of checking in, I asked them to contact my kidney doctor. About an hour after being in the room, my kidney doctor showed up. They started labs and did not show anything, so they said they would have to do more tests and labs. Then, the words you do not like to hear: *You will need to be admitted.*

I was feeling so bad I did not ask any questions. At this point, the only thing they could do was keep the fever under control. Because I was not stable with my walking, I was not allowed to get up and walk the halls.

On day six, the water in the beach picture on the wall began to appear to move. Now, that was the weirdest experience I have

CABBAGE NUMBER SIX - WHERE DID THIS CABBAGE COME FROM?

ever had! All types of specialists were called in to help figure out my diagnosis.

By now, I had even seen two of the four kidney doctors on the team rotation. Remember, I was only in the hospital for seven days for the kidney transplant. By now, I was really getting concerned. It is one thing to have a diagnosis, but it is a different feeling when you do not know what is going on.

By day nine of this particular hospital stay, the third kidney doctor said it was his last day at the hospital. Dr. Hippen would be on rotation the next day. That day, I reached out and asked everyone who could pray to call out Dr. Hippen's name for wisdom and guidance in a diagnosis.

On day ten, Dr. Hippen came into my room and sat down with my chart. I let him know right away that he had been prayed for, and he said he was grateful. He said, "Before I read your chart, I want to hear your story of what is happening." As I explained everything, he took his own notes and then stated he was going to a quiet room to put everything together. Yes, there would be more tests, but he would have something by the next morning. Prayers continued.

The next morning, Dr. Hippen came in with the diagnosis of Addison's Disease. I had never heard of it. Addison's Disease is basically an adrenal insufficiency. We adjusted medicines, and I was educated on what to do in the future. This hospital stay was a total of fourteen days–much longer than the kidney transplant.

Please join me for a glass of lemonade.

Cabbage Number Seven - Find a Way, Make a Way

In the summer of 2015, I was introduced to a program at the YMCA that is specifically for transplant patients. I took advantage of it and signed up for it. It was a special package with a special rate, yet you had so many options.

I was so excited that I took full advantage of all the opportunities. I was exercising and eating healthy, which resulted in the weight coming off and my energy increasing.

The program was working, and I was working on the program. That fall, I was scheduled to go on a beach retreat in South Carolina with the direct sales company I belong to. I was determined to continue my exercise program while I was there.

Well, if you know me, you know I always like to be prepared. Remember, I am a planner. Having said that, I usually have extra bags or big bags when I travel. This trip, I was going to be smart and put everything in one *large* suitcase. Now, you must know I am a five-foot-tall woman with arthritis.

I was not driving, so I had to meet the girls I traveled with. We met, and my daddy put my suitcase in the car trunk. It had wheels, so I was able to roll it out of the house with no problem. Off to the beach we went. They even said on the way, "Wow, Tina, we cannot believe you were able to get all your stuff in one suitcase." I replied, "Me too. I have my tennis shoes to walk on the beach, my exercise clothes, along with my clothes for the retreat all in one suitcase."

We arrived at the resort and went to check-in. Everything was all good. As normal, we unloaded the car close to the entrance with the luggage cart close by. Well, when we—yes, we, no attendant at the entrance—went to pull my suitcase out of the trunk... I fell down. I know that is not a big deal to most, but my bones are very fragile at this point due to steroids. When I fell, I felt something shift in my tailbone.

Now, based on previous experiences, I knew not to move. The ladies I was traveling with said, "Tell us what to do." I coached them on what to do. We were about to use the luggage cart for me to get to the front seat of the car to go to the nearest ER.

We arrived at the ER, and the staff member brought a wheelchair out for me and assisted me. But as the transporter wheeled me in, a lady coming out said, "You better take your jewelry off; they will steal it." I am like, *Oh no, is this a safe place for me to be?* The girl walking with me looked at me, and I said, "Do not leave me."

Even though the pain was in my back and my leg, and the leg had now started swelling, I was mostly concerned about my kidney. I knew I was not having anything done without my kidney doctors. The room was dirty, the trash can was overflowing, the ethics were questionable, and the staff was not working together... I could go on and on.

I started to ask myself, *Who do I know that lives close to the beach and could drive me four hours back home?* I called a family I had not talked to in years! I called friends at home who could drive to pick me up. I had to *get out!*

My next thought was perhaps I could take an ambulance from South Carolina to North Carolina. Did you know it is not like calling a taxi or Uber? At that time, it was not considered medically necessary. All I could think was, *Well, I do not want it to become medically necessary, and that is why I want out of here!*

Of course, my phone went dead, and I did not have a charger. The staff could not even help me to charge my phone. At this point, I was now solo as the girls had gone back to the retreat. The staff did bring me one of the hospital's cordless phones to use as I was still calling people to figure out my escape.

Once I got the phone, I kept the phone. It was my lifeline, for sure. When the staff would come in, I would hide it under the sheets. I was also smart enough to turn the silence mode on. If staff came into the room, they could not hear the phone ring. I needn't have worried because they did not stay in the room long when they did come in. When the phone rang, if it had a 704 area code, I knew it was for me, and I would answer. I let the staff answer the other calls. Find a way, make a way.

Finally, I found an ambulance service that would drive me four hours home. The clencher was that it would be self-pay up front to the tune of $4,000. Remember, I know how to turn cabbage into lemonade... and I just so happened to have an extra charge card just for emergencies! This, in my opinion, was an emergency. I asked the gentleman, "Are you ready for the card number?" Boy, was that an expensive ride home! Sometimes, you have to do what you have to do. The hospital staff was happy when I left since I returned the phone that they could not find.

The ambulance service delivered me to the main trauma hospital in Charlotte, NC, on a Saturday morning at 2:00 AM with lots of action in the ER. Only God would have my dad and aunt in a place where I could see them as I entered! They were even able to go with me to the room! Boy, was I ever so happy to see family!

After more X-rays, it showed I had a fracture in my lower back and a strained muscle in my leg. I was put in a leg splint and followed up with an orthopedic doctor within two weeks. That sounded good to me at this point.

It was October, and I had big plans with my direct sales business. It was time for me to figure out how to take this cabbage and turn it into lemonade. I could not drive, and it was before the virtual world. What was I to do?

Well, I would be going into a lot of doctor's offices. So, I simply decided that I would take my product with me. My dad would push me in my wheelchair, and my aunt would pull my bags with my products to sell. I went to my appointments and let the staff know that after my appointment, I would be set up in the lobby of that floor. Oh my, did I make some sales or what? Talk about taking cabbage and turning it into lemonade. *Meet me in the lobby for some lemonade while you shop.*

Just wait for this story! My orthopedic doctor was in the same building as my kidney doctor. I provided the best customer service, as I would go to each floor on my visits. If I were going to the orthopedic, I would call the front desk of the kidney office and let them know what day I was coming. On the day of the orthopedic appointment, I would call the kidney office on the way to remind them of my appointment. I will say it was a productive holiday season despite the opportunities.

Mark 2:3-5 reads, "And they come unto him, bringing one sick of the palsy, which was borne of four. And when they could not come nigh unto him for the press, they uncovered the roof where he was: and when they had broken it up, they let down the bed wherein the sick of the palsy lay. When Jesus saw their faith, he said unto the sick of the palsy, son thy sins be forgiven thee" (KJV).

Do not allow obstacles to stop your progress! Find a way to reach your goal. If those men could raise a paralyzed man through the roof, you can reach your goal or mission. The process will be different, but you can do it.

Cabbage Number Eight - The Transition

I mentioned her earlier in this story, and there are simply not enough words to describe my mother. My mother was a God-fearing, loving woman who loved to cook. She loved me, and I loved her. My health limitations did not get in the way of me helping her how ever I could after her fall.

She was known for her cooking—especially banana pudding and her twenty-layer chocolate cake. Cake is known among the American Indian community. On one occasion, people thought it was a stack of pancakes because the layers were so thin!

You see, when my mother fell in June of 2011, it started a spiral decline in her health. So, by the time 2016 rolled around, she was in the ER or hospital at least once a month, which continued into 2017. In March 2017, the ER doctor asked me to step into the hallway. The first question she asked was, "How are you doing this?" I replied, "Doing what?"

She asked, "How are you taking care of your mother?" I replied, "I'm still not sure exactly what you mean, but I am taking care of my mother the way she would take care of me." I had no idea where these questions were coming from.

The doctor stated that she didn't see how my father and I were able to take care of her with her health issues. I told her that I didn't know any better; I just did what my mother needed when she needed it done. She told me that my mother's health was significantly declining and that she would be transferred to a hospice facility within a few days. What a shock! This was a load of cabbage I did not like.

This was such a shock for everyone, including all of our family and friends. Of course, when you hear the word "hospice," you think of the very end. My mother spent the next few days in the hospital and was then transported to the hospice house.

My mom's room at the hospice center was always full of visitors. When we arrived, my dad told the staff that we would need extra chairs, and we did. The encouragement and support was always a blessing. The staff shared it was rare to see so much support as they had patients who never had visitors. That is so sad to me. My dad and I both would stay with my mom at night.

At this stage of things, I was adjusting to the time that was coming for my mother to transition. I accepted it and was at peace that she would pass at the hospice house versus our home.

Well, as they say, the fruit doesn't fall far from the tree. My mother had fight and determination in her, too. She was stable within a week and was able to come home for five weeks. During that time, we continued to make memories right up to her passing.

My mother didn't ask for much, so when she did I was on it. She wanted her nails done. That was another trait of hers. Even with her talents in cooking, she maintained healthy, strong nails. About two weeks before her passing, she wanted her nails done. Not just any type of nails; she wanted the gel nails she had started to get. So, what did I do? I found someone to come to our house to do my mom's gel nails. This made her feel so good. That was one of my favorite memories as she gained her wings on May 2, 2017.

I still miss her to this day and do not have one regret about how my life schedule changed. I received comments after her celebration of life that the ceremony was so beautiful and personable. It reminded me that I had taken that load of cabbage and turned it into lemonade in honor of my mother. Let us have a toast of lemonade to my mother, Clementine Hunt, from a crystal pitcher trimmed in gold in a crystal goblet.

How to Live Without My Mom

My mother and I had a close relationship. She was not only my mother, but also my mentor, teacher, friend, shopping buddy, listener, and the list goes on. She was a vital part of teaching me how to overcome. I would tell people, "My momma is the praying one." She would ask God for direction and permission. I am the one who has to ask for God's forgiveness because I would do it without direction and have to ask for forgiveness.

After the funeral services of a loved one, you are no longer on a schedule of places to be or things you have to do. After all of that, reality sets in. Friends stop coming to check on you, and calls of condolences become fewer and farther between. Fortunately, I was once again grateful for my tight-knit group of friends who consistently reached out to me following mom's service, treating me to meals, going on shopping trips, and more.

Make sure to reach out to individuals after they have lost a loved one. This is the moment when the reality of the situation sets in, making it extremely challenging. Emotions can be overwhelming and unpredictable, turning the experience into a tumultuous roller coaster ride. On another note, be careful what you say. It is truly best to say less and just give a hug. There are no words to ease the pain, but that hug goes a long way. I have often said I should write a book about what not to say to someone after a loved one passes.

The beginning of "the firsts" without my momma and entering the new normal phase was hard. Nine days after my mother's passing, it was my birthday. Twelve days after her passing was Mother's Day. To this day, I still have to be careful around that day. Church is the place where mothers are recognized and loved so much on Mother's Day, so I have to distract myself and do something different. No judging, please; remember, everyone handles grief differently.

In June came the first funeral that I needed to attend. *God, please help me!* I was praying, but it got really serious as I started getting dressed. The outfit I was going to wear needed to be hemmed, but I had no time to take it to an alteration person. I instead, purchased some of that sew-in stuff that would give me enough hem for the evening visitation. Why is this a big deal? My momma was a seamstress, and she could hem something up in a quick minute.

I arrived at the home for the visitation. Still not one hundred percent confident about the look and security of this hem, I arrived at the house for the visitation with safety pins. Yes, we were going to pin these legs up. Yep, I did it.

It was just about time the evening was over, and everyone was going home. My friend Mary said, "Tina, let's get a picture together." I replied, "Let me put my lipstick on." You cannot take a picture without fresh lipstick, right? After applying my fresh lipstick, I turned around and fell across the floor face-first. Well, glory! The tip of my shoe had gotten caught in the hem of the pants that had become loose, and *bam*!

First, let me tell you we took the picture with us both sitting on the floor. I also called my kidney doctors and explained what was bruised and what was swelling. They felt it was safe for me to go to a local hospital and not meet them at the Charlotte Trauma Hospital. I called friends to see if they could pick me up as my dad was out of town working. They said *yes* and came. The men at the home picked me up and put me in the car. Remember, I know better than to try and get up after a fall.

We arrived at the hospital, and they wheel-chaired me in. Now let me tell you I was bruised and swelling, thinking my finger was broken. But I was the prettiest thing in the ER that night with my black jumpsuit and pearls. So, I requested a paper pair of scrubs. I knew it would be a charge, but I did not want them to cut my jumpsuit. Because I was dressed up, they were curious about where I had been since I was not drunk.

As we went in for my x-rays, my friend Renee was with me. The technician asked me if that was my mother. Well, that brought about an outburst of tears, and I could not answer her. Renee explained my mother had recently passed, and she was a friend. After a while, I said, "I'm sorry it is still all so fresh."

The results of this fall led to a broken, funny bone that would require surgery. That is not even funny, but it is what it is. Needless to say, I became known as the girl who fell at Rosa's the night before her funeral.

The year of firsts is hard. Thanksgiving and Christmas, especially Christmas for me, as it was my mother's birthday, too. She always said she enjoyed celebrating her birthday on the same day as Jesus. See where I get my glass half-full attitude?

Show compassion towards individuals as they navigate through the first year after the loss of a loved one. Make sure they are not spending holidays alone. Even if they have family, you need to check in on them.

Cabbage Number Nine - What's Happening?

In mid-January of 2021, I began having some chest discomfort, but nothing too bad. Just that feeling like you can zip those jeans, but it doesn't mean that they fit. After six weeks, I noticed it was continuing with no pattern. I decided to see a cardiologist at the end of March, and in April, I started getting tests done to see what was happening. One test result, in particular, showed a 70 to 80% blockage of not one but two of the arteries to the heart. Well, this started moving things fast. By April 20th, I was going in for a heart catheterization. Where in the world did this load of cabbage come from? Let me add here my heart condition was not from poor eating or lifestyle; it was totally hereditary.

This time period happened during COVID-19, so all my hospital procedures and stays were done alone. The only time I could have someone with me was when I could not drive home after procedures, and they would let the driver come in to pick me up.

However, during the procedure for possible stents, not only did I have to go alone, but they also told me to bring an overnight bag. *What?!* I was scared to death as my family dropped me off at the door. Having to walk in all by myself and having no idea what was waiting for me on the other side was a very different experience.

My family dropped me off not even at the front door–it was in a parking deck. I got my overnight bag out of the vehicle, and as I was walking across the over-street walkway, all I could think was, *God, this is worse than any mission trip I have been on.* All I knew to do was to follow the directions and look for the signs on the paper I had been given. I did not know who I was going to meet on the other side of that walkway. *It is just you and me, God. I will have faith and be positive.*

I finally arrived in the right room, still scared, with my emotions all over my face. A gentleman met me at the door and asked my name. I answered him, ending with, "I am scared." He assured me he would take care of me with his part and walk with me to my next stop. I thanked him and said I was grateful.

After paperwork, he took me and others to the elevator. The other people had had this procedure done before, and they were not scared. My new friend took me to the pre-op room. He gave them my full name, including, "She is scared." Pre-op nurses said they would take really good care of me. (Seriously, don't they all say that?) They got all their paperwork and IVs started, and I was ready to get it over with.

In the prep talk, they let me know they would call my contact person every step of the way. My contact person was my best friend, as my dad was struggling in the wake of my mother's death. I felt too much stress knowing I was by myself. As they finished, I heard them call Jill.

I was now in the "hurry up and wait" stage of the procedure. I had brought a book along to pass the time, but it's a little hard to read and highlight things with an IV in your arm. But I have no fear–I could still talk. So, I would call the staff over to my bed to chat. Remember, my unofficial last name is "I am scared." Then, they got busy and had to attend to other patients. Moving right along to the next opportunity, I called Jill on the phone to make sure they had actually been calling her as they had claimed.

The staff said they would get me in ten minutes, so we hung up. As so often happens in the hospital, the unexpected happened. Another patient who had just come from his heart catheterization surgery (just what I was waiting to have done!) started coding. Read: That means his heart stopped! This all happened just out of my range of sight, but I could see enough and hear the panic.

Well, glory be, guess who was next to go back? Yes, it was my turn. Once again, I let them know I was scared and I just experienced the code blue with the gentleman. Of course, they apologized that I had to experience that right before my catheterization. Now, I really wanted my family and friends. Needless to say, my blood pressure had just gone up a notch.

Thankfully, everyone was nice and kept me calm through the catheterization process. They do not put you to sleep for this procedure. Because of the extra events that happened before I went in, I did ask for extra numbing medicine. Then, five minutes later, they said we were done.

I was excited until they showed me the x-ray. The x-ray showed that it was worse than we thought, and stents were not an option. So, the plus was now I needed a ride home after laying flat for several hours. The not-so-good news was I needed to see a surgeon soon. Before discharge, I was scheduled to see a heart surgeon the next day.

After a 45-minute visit with the heart surgeon the next day, my surgery was scheduled for April 30, 2021. What do you know… My 55th birthday party in May had just been canceled by a man I had just met. Why wait, right? He was the best surgeon ever–he had no notes, computer, or anything when he entered the room. He thoroughly went over the reasons for doing it sooner rather than later. Once again, God gave me ten days to plan and prepare.

The Heart of Faith over Fear

During my quiet time the next morning, April 22, 2021, as I was reading God's Word, I read Psalm 112:6-8, "Surely the righteous will never be shaken, they will be remembered forever. They will have no fear of bad news; their hearts are steadfast, trusting in the Lord. Their hearts are secure, they will have no fear in the end, they will look in triumph on their foes" (NIV). After reading this I had peace about the surgery. I chose to have faith over fear. This would end up being my Scripture for this event. I printed out several copies on pink paper of the Scripture and took them with me for the surgery.

Now that I had God's word and peace, I worked on my physical body. I wanted my lungs to be strong for this surgery. I thought it was important because of my compromised immune system and that I would be on the ventilator for some time during and after surgery. The question was, what can I do to make it better for me? Sometimes, we must take full responsibility for a better outcome.

One of my Diva nurse friends, Melanie, suggested to build my lungs I use the spirometer. So, every two hours from 10 AM to 10 PM, for five minutes, I used the spirometer. I even carried it with me in the car if it was time for a spirometer.

Friday, April 30, 2021, I rolled up to the hospital at 5:00 AM with my dad and best friend. The surgery was scheduled for 7:30 AM, and due to COVID-19, only one person was allowed to stay.

> *Sometimes, we must take full responsibility for a better outcome.*

The possibility of only one person being allowed to accompany me had been previously discussed, and since my dad was over 80 years old and not as good with medical terms as my best friend, we decided to have her stay instead of him. She was better equipped with knowing what questions to ask during and after the surgery.

What a thrill when you have to be somewhere early to wait. There was not a lot going on in the hospital at 5:00 AM, but my friend and I found a spot to sit and wait. When they called me back to my room, the only thing I had with me was my Scripture and my cellphone. To be honest, that was a very long walk to the pre-op room. Once the nurse started, it was busy for about an hour. I let her know in my pre-op workup that I had used the spirometer for the past ten days to build my lungs up.

Then we started the waiting game again. Can I mention here there was no cell reception? I couldn't even play on my phone or scroll Facebook early in the morning. I suppose it was meant for me to be in a peaceful, calm, and prayerful frame of mind.

I shared the verses from Psalm 112:6-8 and my faith over fear words with everyone who came into my room. I felt like I had an army of prayer warriors praying for me every time I shared those verses. One nurse even stopped, looked at me, and said, "Thank you. That means a lot." I had to get permission from the anesthesiologist to carry my Scripture with me on the gurney, but I wanted God's Word with me on the bed. My Scripture was printed on pink paper so it would stand out. Who would say no to God's Word and Tina, right?

We were finally off to the operating room at about 10:30 AM. The surgeon arrived at the same time, and I told him he was late for the party. I do not remember much after that. They seem to knock me out quickly when I go in talking. The next thing I remember was waking up with a sore throat the next day in the ICU and seeing all the tubes, wires, etc. The nurses let me know everything went great. They always say that, right?

I was reassured when my dad and best friend arrived in my room, and she confirmed that everything had gone well. The doctor fixed the blockages and even found an aneurysm. Well, glory! The surgeon had taken care of everything, and we were still on plan. The nurse shared with my dad and best friend when they arrived that they were able to take me off the ventilator six hours early. Well, glory again!

The plan was for me to be in the ICU for three to four days and in the hospital for a total of seven to ten days due to my compromised immune system. But God...

Let me break down God's plan to you:

Friday – Surgery
Saturday – ICU

Sunday – Step down from the ICU room
Monday – You can go home tomorrow
Tuesday – I went home. Well, glory! I love God's plan so much better.

When I shared the news with my dad and best friend, they both said they were not ready for me to come home. There were still a few things needed, such as a schedule of people to stay with me when I came home. To which I replied, "I have faith in you both so that you can figure it out." And they did! I was so ready to get out of the hospital that I came home in the hospital gown. I did not wait for my friend to bring me clothes; instead, I called her and let her know I would meet her at the hospital entrance. Cheers with a glass of lemonade!

During my stay, I continued to share my faith over the fear mindset and the Scripture. My kidney doctors were not surprised at my quick stay, for they knew my faith and my positive mindset. The nurses, however, were very surprised by my quick stay. This gave me an opportunity to share the goodness of God along with my faith and also how I had to do my part of believing and doing my breathing exercises.

The hospital staff could not believe we had a schedule for people to visit. I explained I normally have a room full of people when I am in the hospital. Because I like to have fun, and since visitors were limited, when the nurses got a break, they would come to my room. One night, I had to ask for something to help me sleep, but they still came in, thinking I would be able to talk with them.

Of course, it was about a year of recovery after this surgery with a three-month program of heart rehab. I had a tremendous amount of soreness from the surgery and a lot of work to do to build my strength up. The surgeon was impressed and proud. His office sent me a birthday card and told me I was his poster child, for I had raised the bar very high for future patients. My classmates from high school came to my house and had a flash mob birthday celebration in my yard on the day my birthday party was to take place.

As I started writing this book, it is September 8, 2023, and I am two years out from my heart surgery and eleven years out from my kidney transplant. I have had no major complications from the heart surgery. Well, glory! Just so you know, I have had lots of other medical surgeries, including but not limited to gallbladder removal, two hand surgeries, a stomach ulcer, and a dislocated hip, just to name a few. The ones I shared are just the highlights.

Would you please join me in the east wing of the estate in the formal parlor at 5:00 PM for some lemonade? The dress attire will be all things sparkly.

Make Some Lemonade

This was a recount of my brief journey through my major life obstacles/opportunities. My prayer is that you have been encouraged. My life saying is that *God gave me cabbage and told me to make lemonade because lemons to lemonade would be too easy.* You see, to have a testimony, you must go through a test. In life, we might not always have the best ingredients to work with, but God has given us what He knows we can use. Your faith and testimony will be stronger through it all.

This book was written to inspire you to be an overcomer and to know that God has a purpose for your life. None of us get in a car to drive to our vacation spot without planning and packing. We also know we will not get all the green lights on the road. Life can be about the same. We plan, but there will be some red lights and some yellow lights, along with the green lights.

Who knows, sometimes a light could come on the dashboard of your car in the middle of nowhere, letting you know you need to address something. I don't know about you, but I don't know what all those symbols on my car dash mean! But I do know if I can get to a dealership, they will know. Imagine this: you arrive at the car service center, and the technicians have left. You are an hour away from home. You pray some more, and then around the corner comes a receptionist in the service area who is familiar with the symbols. She takes the keys and says, "Come with me. I will reset it and show you how to do it." Five minutes later, the unknown lighted symbol is gone. It's good to go, and you drive the hour home.

As I am about to leave, I have some products in my car that I can give to these ladies. They thanked me and asked for a book from my company because they wanted to order from me. You see, had the unknown light not come on, I would have probably never met these two ladies who became customers of mine.

Yes, this is another true story of mine. This literally happened to me this week. It is simply turning the cabbage into lemonade. By the way, I did celebrate my 55th birthday; it was celebrated in September instead of May, and boy, did we have a lot to celebrate. Again, I am thankful for the goodness of God.

When problems come your way, remember to pause, pray, pivot, and look for a positive perspective. Thank you for spending some time with me. Let's meet at the lemonade stand, giving God our praises.

When problems come your way, remember to pause, pray, pivot, and look for a positive perspective.

In closing, I want to share some stories, including Bible stories, that have helped me in this journey called life.

Do Not Judge by What You See

Throughout my journey of making this lemonade out of cabbage, I have never wanted to be defined or labeled as having a disability or what the world calls obstacles. Remember, I call them opportunities.

You see, so many times, I have been judged or labeled for things. Along with those labels have come with what I call bullying. There were times when I would get attention for my courage or don't-give-in spirit. People have made statements like, "I know you like getting all this attention."

When I was on chemo for about eighteen months, and my hair was falling out, I was upset and cried one day (because remember, a woman's hair is her glory). Someone said to me, "You are not the first person to lose your hair, and you will not be the last." Yes… I call that bullying.

How about the time I parked in a handicapped spot as I was recovering from my kidney transplant surgery? A man walked by and said, "You are not handicapped." Just because something is not visible to you or to the naked eye, that doesn't mean there is not something internally going on. I simply walked past this one.

One time, I remember parking in a handicapped spot after both knee surgeries, remembering at the same time that I had not driven in over a year, and I was super excited! As I pulled into the parking spot, I noticed a man and woman coming out of the store. My mother was with me, and I said, "Momma, that man is going to say something about me parking here." My godly mother said, "Ignore him, Tina." She always taught me to ignore drama and ignorance. This time, I just was not feeling it.

We got out of my car. The man was behind my car and directed his comment to me. "You know you are not handicapped and should not be parking there." I then replied, "Would you like to see my knees from my double knee surgery at the same time? Or would you like to pay the balance after my surgery?" He immediately stopped talking and walked to his car.

I guess you might say, I wanted to get the last word in. So, I shared with him, "The next time you think about making a comment or questioning someone's actions, remember me."

Of course, my momma said, "Tina, I taught you better." I replied, "Momma, I know, but sometimes it is hard not to respond back. It is not like I enjoy parking close, especially as a young person, but if I don't, I will not make it through the store." She agreed.

I believe that if someone possesses a handicap placard, it has been approved by a physician for a specific purpose. If the person is using it or somebody else's handicap placard illegally, then they are responsible for those actions, not me. I don't have to answer for them.

Broken For A Purpose

A woman was in the store with two kids and a long line: one big kid and one toddler. The big kid had a bag of glow sticks, and the toddler was screaming for them. So, the mom opened the pack and gave the toddler a stick, which stopped the tears. The toddler was now a happy camper and smiling. Right as they were about to walk outside, the big kid took the glow stick and bent it. Well, that led to the toddler screaming again. The mom was about to start fussing, and the big kid gave it back to the toddler. Walking outside, the toddler noticed that the stick was now glowing, and his brother said, "I had to break it so you could get the full effect from it." Author Unknown

Have you ever thought God had to break you and me to show us why He created us? We had to be broken to fulfill God's purpose. The toddler was happy just swinging the "unbroken" glow stick because he did not understand what it was to do, which was to glow. There are some people who will be content just "being," but there are some of us that God has chosen who have to be broken. What is your perspective on your brokenness? Maybe it's time to glow for God.

Genesis 25:26 reads, ... "and after that came his brother out, and his hand took hold on Esau's heel; and his name was called Jacob: and Isaac was three score years old when she bare them" (KJV). Jacob was a leader made usable through brokenness. Gifted and natural leaders can have a difficult time, especially with character issues. Jacob, no matter what he did or where he went, stirred things up. Over time, his leadership created prosperity.

> *What is your perspective on your brokenness? Maybe it's time to glow for God.*

"Therefore, the children of Israel eat not of the sinew which shrank, which is upon the hollow of the thigh, "unto this day: because he touched the hollow of Jacob's thigh in the sinew that shrank" (Genesis 32:32 KJV).

However, a leader who goes his own way, doing his own thing, and seeking his own benefits cannot be an effective instrument in God's hands. God had to break Jacob to make him useful. Sometimes we have to be broken. When you are standing in a trial or adversity, you are being prepared to serve God better.

Remember, it is the valleys that connect the mountains.

RESOURCES

Supporting a Friend or Family Member

The book is written based on my journey and my experience. A couple of times, I have referred to my family and friend support, but I wanted to elaborate a little more, as I was specifically asked this question recently. As a mother, father, and family, what do we do when our young loved one has been given a diagnosis that can possibly change or alter their lifestyle? How do we answer the questions? How do we discuss it?

First, as a parent, I would suggest assuring your loved one that the diagnosis will not define the individual. The enemy wants us to be labeled individuals, and that is not true. Psalm 139:14 says, "I will praise thee; for I am fearfully and wonderfully made: marvellous are thy works; and that my soul knoweth right well" (KJV).

Next, you want to listen and be available; be all-in-present. More than likely, there will be tons of questions and negative statements, such as: *What did I do? Does God not love me? I'll never be able to get married? My life is over with this diagnosis? And oftentimes, for females, I'll never have children.*

So you want to listen intently. Will you have all the answers? Of course not! But the support of listening is huge, and it's an opportunity for your loved one to release things that they shouldn't have to let build up inside. Listening will show your loved one that you care.

You will want to get the family involved. Maybe have a family meeting and allow your loved one to share and the family to ask questions. Again, getting it out. You can write these down and ask the doctor. It's also a time for the family to show support, letting the loved one know they are not in it alone. Family stands for unit. The unit stands for You and I together.

For me, even though I was the one going through everything, my parents were compassionate and showed that they cared. For example, if I had a test and I couldn't eat, my parents didn't eat in front of me. When I had to give up salt, my mom quit cooking with salt, and my dad would add his own salt. Your loved one will still want to be as independent as possible. So, even though you might want to do everything for them, try to let them be independent. But, if you see them truly struggling with something, you can jump in to help or offer your assistance. For me I struggle with asking for help. Do you remember me trying to get the suitcase out of the trunk and the suitcase won? It's nice when I'm struggling, and someone walks up and says, "I'll do that." Remember to treat others the way you want to be treated. You can do this for anyone, I think. It goes along with being kind.

One last thing: I hate to mention this, but bullying happens. Yes, as a teenager, there is a strong possibility this could happen. Teenagers who have not been exposed to a family with health challenges, whether visible or not, do not know how to respond.

Since we cannot control them, let's look at what we have control over and how we can handle it.

The first lesson to learn is that your true friends will not make fun of you. The so-called friends will be gone. Your true friends will be supportive and understanding. Know that when you are questioned about your health, you do not have to give any or all of the information. I have found that less is best. What do I mean? Give short answers like, "I have some health challenges." Or if it's at the very beginning, you can say, "I don't have a confirmed diagnosis." Remember you did not have to give them all the details.

I will leave you with this one last thing. It's okay to see a counselor. We have to talk and release these feelings and or ask the question.

Know that these suggestions are for all. It's hard as a teenager and as an adult. Remember, you can do hard things. You are strong! Keep your mindset on positive and encouraging things.

Becoming An Organ Donor

If you would like more information on becoming an organ donor, this section is for you! First, as a kidney recipient, let me say *Thank you!* There are a couple of ways to register to be an organ donor. You can register when you get your driver's license, or you can go to www.registerme.org, which is the national registry link. Make sure to discuss your decision with your family so that they know your wishes.

How to Pray for a Personal Relationship with Christ

As you read the book, you might have asked yourself, *How can I have a personal relationship with Jesus Christ?* Or maybe you are not sure about your relationship with Jesus. Simply going to church, being good, saying, "My grandmother was a Christian," etc., is not salvation. Knowing you are not saved is the first step to getting saved. There is a huge difference between religion and relationship, similar to if you are traveling and realize you cannot stay on the road you are on to get to the proper destination. So, how do you have that personal relationship?

The best resource of all is the Bible–let's go there to find the answer. Romans 3:23 says, *For all have sinned and come short of the glory of God.* This means everyone who has ever been born has sinned. What is sin? Sin is anything that we do that is wrong or against God's standard of holiness. When we know what we are supposed to do and we choose not to do it, that makes it sinful. God cannot allow unholiness into His presence in heaven. But wait –the good news is coming!

Romans 5:8 says, "But God commendeth his love toward us, in that, while we were yet sinners, Christ died for us" (KJV). Here's the good news: God sent His only son, Jesus, to die for our sins on the cross of Calvary. Jesus was perfect, holy, and sinless; his death atoned for our sins.

Romans 6:23 says, "For the wages of sins is death, but the gift of God is eternal life through Jesus Christ our Lord" (KJV). Let me ask you something. Have you ever gone to great expense and lengths to purchase someone a special gift? The only thing they needed to do was come to you to receive and accept it. Yet, the person never came to receive the gift. Did the person receive the gift? No. Jesus died for each of us, but we must choose to come and receive it. As I said at the beginning, you must realize you are lost and then realize you need Jesus.

To receive this free gift of salvation, keep reading. The best is yet to come...

Romans 10:9-10 says, "That if thou shalt confess with the mouth the Lord Jesus, and shalt believe in thine heart that God hath raised Him from the dead, thou shalt be saved. For with the heart, man believeth unto righteousness; and with the mouth, confession is made unto salvation" (KJV).

Romans 10:13 says, "For whosoever shall call upon the name of the Lord shall be saved" (KJV). These verses show us exactly what we need to do to get saved. First, confess that you are a sinner and that you need to get saved. Next, you need to believe that Jesus is the Son of God who died on the cross and rose again so that you can be saved. Last, just ask Him to forgive you of your sins, come into your heart, and save you. That is it! According to Scripture, that is how to receive Jesus as your personal Savior. If you would like to do that, pray something like the prayer below. Remember, it's not the prayer but the meaning of it from your heart.

Dear Jesus, I confess that I am a sinner. I know that I myself cannot go to heaven. Lord, I believe you died for me. You were buried and rose again for me. I believe you came to take the sin of the world, and that includes me. Jesus, come into my heart, save me. Make me pure, make me clean, and make me whole. Jesus, thank you for coming into my heart. Help me live a life consecrated to you and a life as a light for you. In Jesus's name, I pray.

My heart rejoices at this decision you have made! This is the most important decision of all. Next, you will want to join the fellowship in a Bible-believing and Bible-teaching church to help you grow in your walk with the Lord.

If you would like to know more, you can go to my website, www.cabbage2lemonade.com, and click on the Saved tab.

CABBAGE TO LEMONADE?

Tina's ABCs of Positive vs Negative Words

A Anxious ⟶ Achiever
B Battles ⟶ Blessings
C Crisis ⟶ Christ
D Doubt ⟶ Dream
E Earthworm ⟶ Eagle
F Fear ⟶ Faith
G Greedy ⟶ Grateful
H Hurtful ⟶ Helpful
I Ignorant ⟶ Integrity
J Jealous ⟶ Joyful
K Kind-less ⟶ Kind
L Lazy ⟶ Love
M Mindless ⟶ Mindful
N Never ⟶ Now
O Obstacle ⟶ Opportunity
P Panic ⟶ Prayer
Q Quantity ⟶ Quality
R Reject ⟶ Receive
S Sinner ⟶ Saved
T Trial ⟶ Testimony
U Unworthy ⟶ Union
V Victim ⟶ Victory
W Worry ⟶ Worship
e**X**cel in **Y**our **Z**est for life

RESOURCES

So, You Think God Can't Use You?!

The next time you feel like God can't use you, remember the following people:

Noah was a drunk...

Abraham was too old...

Isaac was a daydreamer...

Jacob was a liar...

Leah was ugly...

Joseph was abused...

Moses couldn't talk...

Gideon was afraid...

Samson had long hair and was a womanizer...

Rahab was a prostitute...

Jeremiah and Timothy were too young...

David had an affair and was a murderer...

Elijah was suicidal...

CABBAGE TO LEMONADE?

Jonah ran from God…

Naomi was a widow…

Job went bankrupt…

John the Baptist ate bugs…

Peter denied Christ…

The Disciples fell asleep while praying…

Martha worried about everything…

Mary Magdalene was demon-possessed…

The Samaritan woman was divorced…more than once!

Zaccheus was too small…

Paul was too religious…

Timothy had an ulcer…

And Lazarus was DEAD!

(Author Unknown)

RESOURCES

Pray Until Something Happens

Recently, I heard a saying: God gives His battles to His strongest soldiers. Well, I've heard this in different seasons of my life. Some of my personal replies have been: "God, you have soldiers stronger than me," "God, can you please find someone else to make strong?", "God, I'm strong enough over here," just to name a few. Then, I was reminded that God trusted me with the hard work because I'd give Him praise in the end. He has people watching to see how I, as a Christian, handle things; when I am weak, He is strong.

All of this reminds me of the song "God is in this Story" by Big Daddy Weave and Katy Nichole.[1] The song speaks of the broken parts, the addiction, the disease, depression, broken homes, the storms of life, and the list goes on. We must remember He never leaves us, and He holds our hearts in His hands. We must trust in Jesus and keep our eyes on Him. Have you ever seen a runner looking down as they are running a marathon? No, they are looking up. When you are looking down, you are setting yourself up to stumble and fall. At least when you are looking up, you are more capable of following the path God has for you.

Remember to PUSH: Pray Until Something Happens.

---

[1] Katy Nichole. "Katy Nichole & Big Daddy Weave - 'God Is In This Story' (Official Music Video)," n.d. https://www.youtube.com/watch?v=ryD3D9X2myk.

Tina's Recipes

My 5-ingredient Cabbage Soup Recipe

1 head of cabbage, chopped
1 chopped onion
1 small bag of carrots
1 small bag of frozen lima beans
1 small bag of frozen green beans
Season to taste with minced garlic powder and
 Mrs. Dash's seasoning

Instructions:

Put all of the ingredients into a pot, then fill ¾ full of water. Cook slowly for 3-4 hours or until done, stirring occasionally. Sometimes, I will double the recipe. You can also add fresh boneless chicken breast to give it a little boost of protein.

Festive Lemonade: Cranberry Pineapple Punch

This is what I serve at major celebrations. This is very good; I always make a double batch and backup to refill. Everyone likes this one!

3 cups (24 oz.) 100% Dole Canned Pineapple Juice, Chilled
3 cups (24 oz.) Cranberry Juice Cocktail, Chilled
4 cups Ginger Ale
1/2 cup fresh or frozen cranberries
Ice

Pineapple Lemonade

This is a great summertime lemonade. You can use fresh fruit, but then you'll need to add ice for it to be chilled enough.

1 cup of Country Time lemonade mix
1 46 oz can of chilled pineapple juice
2 small bags of frozen strawberries
1 small bag of frozen pineapples
Two cans of Sprite
Mix all together and chill. Serve over ice.

ABOUT THE AUTHOR

Tina Hunt was diagnosed with a not-so-familiar disease at the age of 17, her senior year in high school. She has learned to overcome and be positive during any crisis. Her motto has been that *God gave her cabbage and instructed her to make lemonade because lemons to lemonade would have been too easy.* Thus, she has acquired the ability to do so simply by transforming cabbage into lemonade.

Among Tina's many interests is spending time in nature, which she enjoys doing (while, of course, protecting herself from the sun with sunscreen). She enjoys the sounds of the waves from the beach and the stillness of the mountains. She enjoys being with people, so at almost any given time, she is part of planning an event. She strongly holds the belief that leaders are avid readers, and she is consistently absorbed in a book.

Through her direct sales business, she also helps women with color and skin challenges. She is an ambassador for Donate Life America, where she shares her story of her kidney transplant and encourages others to become organ donors. She is faithful and active in her church.

Her hope is that this book will give people hope and encouragement. It might not always look pretty or even possible, but God can take that cabbage and turn it into lemonade.

If you have been blessed by this book, please share the message with others by posting on social media using #cabbage2lemonade

Website: www.cabbage2lemonade.com
YouTube: www.youtube.com/@tinahunt3267
www.linkedin.com/in/tinahuntmknsd/
https://www.marykay.com/tina2008
www.facebook.com/tina.hunt.7

www.ingramcontent.com/pod-product-compliance
Lightning Source LLC
Chambersburg PA
CBHW032128090426
42743CB00007B/511